Super Predators
POLAR BEARS

TJ Rob

Super-Predators: Polar Bears
By TJ Rob

Copyright Text TJ Rob, 2017

All rights reserved. No part of the book may be reproduced in any form without permission in writing from the author. Reviewers may quote brief passages in review.

Disclaimer

No part of this book may be reproduced in any form or by any means, mechanical or electronic, including photocopying or recording, or by an information storage and retrieval system, or transmitted by email without permission in writing from the publisher. This book is for entertainment purposes only. The views expressed are those of author alone.

Published by:
TJ Rob
Suite 609
440-10816 Macleod Trail SE
Calgary, AB T2J 5N8 www.TJRob.com

ISBN 978-1-988695-53-2

Photo Credits: Images used under license from Flickr.com, Pixabay.com, Public Domain, Wikimedia Commons:
Cover page, Ansgar Walk CC-BY- CC BY 2.5 / via Wikimedia Commons; Back Page, 958187 / Pixabay.com; pg. 1, Ansgar Walk CC BY 2.5 / via Wikimedia Commons; pg. 2, Noel_Bauza / Pixabay.com; pg. 3, Noel_Bauza / Pixabay.com; pg. 4, flickrfavorites / Flickr.com; pg. 5, tskirde /Pixabay.com; pg. 6, Clker-Free-Vector-Images / Pixabay.com; pg. 7, Clker-Free-Vector-Images / Pixabay.com; pg. 8, Martina Mang / Pixabay.com; pg. 9, Colin Knowles / Flickr.com; pg. 9, OpenClipart-Vectors / Pixabay.com; pg. 10, Alan Wilson CC BY SA 3.0 / via Wikimedia Commons; pg. 11, PatternPictures / Pixabay.com; pg. 12, Javallma / Pixabay.com; pg. 13, Christopher Michel / Flikr.com; pg. 14, Christopher Michel / Flikr.com; pg. 15, Christopher Michel / Flikr.com; pg. 16, Kingfisher CC BY-SA 3.0 / via Wikimedia Commons; pg. 16, NOAA / Public Domain via Wikimedia Commons; pg. 16, Andreas Trepte CC BY-SA 2.5 / via Wikimedia Commons; pg. 16, Alastair Rae / Flickr.com; pg. 17, Olsen Dave, U.S. Fish and Wildlife Service / Public Domain via Wikimedia Commons; pg. 18, Lutz Fischer-Lamprecht BY-SA 3.0 / via Wikimedia Commons; pg. 19, Karilop517 / Flickr.com; pg. 19, Gellinger / Pixabay.com; pg. 20, MaxPixel's contributors / Public Domain; pg. 20, Clker-Free-Vector-Images / Pixabay.com; pg. 21, Anita Ritenour / Flickr.com; pg. 22, Oksanna Briere / Pexels.com; pg. 23, foagyleaves / Pixabay.com; pg. 24, Ted / Flickr.com; pg. 24, Christopher Michel / Flickr.com; pg. 25, skeezehurricane0 / Pixabay.com; pg. 26, Russian Academy of Sciences The Polar Bear Program; pg. 26, Ansgar Walk; pg. 27, beingmyself / Flickr.com; pg. 28, Matheus Swanson David Jenkins Polar Bear Pics of Day; pg. 29, beingmyself / Flickr.com; pg. 29, tableatny / Flickr.com; pg. 30, Don O'Brien / Flickr.com; pg. 31, Christopher Michel / Flickr.com; pg. 32, Christopher Michel / Flickr.com; pg. 33, Lucie Provencher / Flickr.com; pg. 34, Christopher Michel / Flickr.com; pg. 35, Christopher Michel / Flickr.com; pg. 36, Tom Pavel / Flickr.com; pg. 36, ChaosHusky / Flickr.com; pg. 37, Christopher Michel / Flickr.com; pg. 38, Clker-Free-Vector-Images / Pixabay.com; pg. 38, Jay Ruzesky / Pexels.com; pg. 39, Brandon Moore / Flickr.com

TABLE OF CONTENTS

	Page
What are Polar Bears?	4
The Origin of Polar Bears	5
Where do Polar Bears live today?	6
How many Polar Bears are left in the wild?	8
How big is a Polar Bear?	9
Are Polar Bears really white?	10
Polar Bear Fur	11
Polar Bear Skin	12
How long do Polar Bears live?	13
Hunting	14
What do Polar Bears like to eat?	16
How often do Polar Bears hunt? How much do they eat?	17
Communication and Sounds Polar Bears make	18
7 Cool Polar Bear Facts	20
Polar Bear Senses	21
Sharp Teeth - Powerful Bite	23
GIANT Paws and Claws	24
Polar Bear Cubs	26
Do All Polar Bears Hibernate?	30
Are Polar Bears good swimmers?	31
Polar Bears are solitary animals	32
How much do Polar Bears sleep?	33
How have Polar Bears adapted to their environment?	34
Polar Bears like to keep clean	36
Polar Bears are Athletes	37
More Cool Polar Bear Facts	38
Human Threats	39
Please leave a review / OTHER books by TJ Rob	40

What are Polar Bears?

Polar Bears are the largest land carnivores in the world. Only the Kodiak Bears of Southern Alaska are similar in size.

Although Polar Bears are related to the Brown Bear, they have evolved over time to live in the freezing Northern Arctic.

Polar Bears are considered Marine Mammals - just like Seals, Whales and Dolphins.

Their Latin name is "Ursus Maritimus" means "Sea Bear".

The Origin of Polar Bears

The best we know today is that Polar Bears evolved between 500,000 and 6 million years ago.

Scientists believe that Polar Bears and Brown Bears evolved from a common ancestor. Because Brown Bears and Polar Bears are closely related they are able to interbreed.

Where do Polar Bears live today?

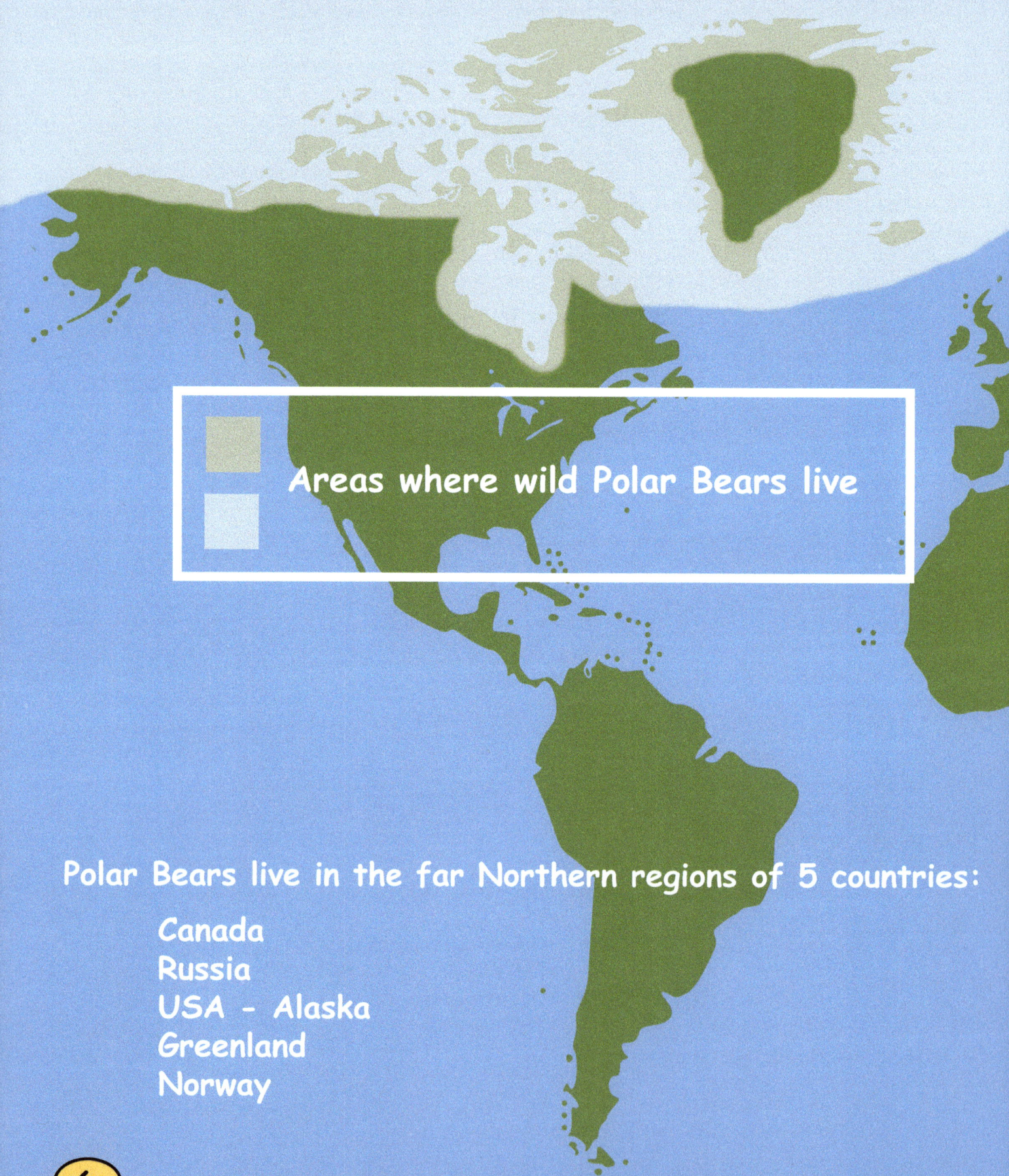

Areas where wild Polar Bears live

Polar Bears live in the far Northern regions of 5 countries:

Canada
Russia
USA - Alaska
Greenland
Norway

About 60% of all Polar Bears on Earth are found in Canada.

Polar Bears only live above or near the Arctic Circle, close to the North Pole.

Polar Bears do not live near the South Pole or in Antarctica.

How many Polar Bears are left in the wild?

Today there are an estimated 20,000 - 35,000 Polar Bears that roam the Arctic.

In the 1950s there were very few laws preventing the hunting of Polar Bears. At that time there were only 6,000 Polar Bears. Since then, most countries have banned Polar Bear hunting and the numbers have grown over the last 60 years.

The numbers of Polar Bears may drop down again in the future as the Arctic climate warms and there is less ice.

How big is a Polar Bear?

Adult male Polar Bears (called boars) are huge, the heaviest of them weighing as much as 1,500 pounds (680 kg). The females (called sows) are smaller, the largest weighing about 750 pounds (340 kg).

Even the smaller sow is 3.75 times heavier than an average man weighing 200 pounds (90 kg).

Male polar bears may grow 10 feet (3 m) tall and females reach about 7 feet (2.13 m) tall - quite a bit taller than the average man.

Polar Bear dimensions by the numbers

Height: 10 feet (3 m) tall.

Weight: 1,500 pounds (680 kg)

Are Polar Bears really White?

Despite what we think, a Polar Bear's fur is not white. Each hair is a clear hollow tube. Polar Bears look white because each hollow hair reflects the light.

Technically speaking, Polar Bear fur is colorless. Each strand of fur is see-through and pigment-free with a hollow core. This reflects light right down to the skin, giving the impression of being white in certain lights.

Polar Bear Fur

Polar Bears are completely covered in fur. Only their noses and footpads do not have fur.

A Polar Bear's coat is really 2 coats in 1. They have a thick, woolly layer of underhair about 1 - 2 inches (2.5 to 5 cm) thick. This is their main insulating layer. Above the underhair layer is a thinner fur layer of stiff, shiny and hollow guard hairs. Guard hairs may be as long as 6 inches (15 cm) long.

The guard hairs look white because of their highly reflective quality. Oils from the seals that the Polar Bear eats can make the hairs look yellow or brown.

Polar Bears molt (shed and replace their fur) every year, in May or June. The molt can last a few weeks. They molt as the weather gets warmer for them to keep their body temperatures cooler. Polar Bears look whitest when they are clean and especially just after they have molted.

Polar Bear Skin

Polar Bears have black skin. The black skin soaks up the sun's heat and helps them stay warm. Even their tongues are dark in color - ranging from blue, to purple and sometimes black.

Polar Bears also have a 4 inch (10.16 cm) layer of fat underneath their skins. This prevents any heat loss from their skins. It works so well that if you looked at a Polar Bear with an infrared camera, the Bear is close to invisible - not giving off any heat. It is as if Polar Bears have a built-in cloak of invisibility.

With such excellent insulation their body temperature won't change even when temperatures reach -34°F (-37°C).

The Seals that Polar Bears love to eat are 50% fat. The high fat content from the blubber of Seals is full of energy that the Polar Bears burn up to stay warm in the freezing Arctic temperatures.

Purple Tongue

How long do Polar Bears live?

On average Polar Bears live to 18 years in the wild.

In captivity, they live longer, with some living to 30 years or more. The longest recorded life span in captivity was 42 years.

Hunting

In the Fall, a Seal cuts 10 to 15 breathing holes in the ice, using the sharp claws on its front flippers.

Seals keep their breathing holes open all winter long, even in ice up to 6 feet (1.83 m) thick. They use these holes to breathe, coming up to the surface every 5 to 15 minutes. They don't always use the same hole.

Polar Bears wait for a Seal to come up through one of these holes. The Bear then attacks the surfacing Seal. Polar Bears have to be very patient because the wait can be very long - sometimes hours, or even days.

Polar Bears find the Seals with their powerful sense of smell.

Waiting by the water

Jumping across the ice

Sometimes Polar Bears stalk their prey. A Bear may see a Seal lying near its breathing hole and stalk it slowly waiting for the best moment to charge.

Polar Bears kill their prey by biting its head or grabbing it with its huge claws. They also may swat their prey with their massive paws.

A Polar Bear may also hunt by swimming beneath the ice.

Seals are the only food source with a high enough fat content and enough calories to keep a Polar Bear healthy. Because they rely on Seals for their main source of food, Polar Bears depend on the sea ice. Less sea ice means fewer Seals and a shortage of high nutrition food.

In Summer, when ice flows retreat, most Polar Bears follow the ice. Sometimes they travel hundreds of kilometers to stay near their food source. During this time, Polar Bears feed on anything that is edible, including birds, eggs, rodents and berries.

What do Polar Bears like to Eat?

Polar Bears feed on meat, particularly Seals.

Ringed Seals are the most commonly found Seal in the Arctic. They are also the easiest to hunt, particularly for female Polar Bears and younger Polar Bears.

Male Polar Bears also hunt the larger Bearded Seals and Harbor Seals.

When an adult Bear is healthy and in good shape, Polar Bears often eat only the blubber (fat) of the Seals they catch. They leave the rest of the carcass for scavengers such as Arctic Foxes, Ravens, and other Bears.

How often do Polar Bears hunt? How much do they eat?

A Polar Bear has a very big stomach. This huge stomach allows the Bear to eat 150 pounds (68 kg) of food in a single sitting. That is like eating more than 500 McDonalds burgers all at once!

In order to maintain its huge size, a Polar Bear must eat the equivalent of 1 Seal every 8 to 10 days.

Polar Bears are willing to share their food with guests. If his Polar Bear guests beg properly, the host Polar Bear will share his catch. A Polar Bear begs for food by approaching low to the ground, slowly circling around the carcass, and touching the nose of the Polar Bear host.

A Polar Bear feeding

Communication and Sounds Polar Bears make

Polar Bears communicate with both sounds and body language.

They use sounds like hissing or growling to show their moods or emotions.

They also use body language to let other Bears know their intentions.

Young Bears or cubs make more noise than adult Polar Bears.

Common cub noises include: squalls, hisses, lip smacks, whimpers and throat rumbles. An adult Polar Bear makes noise to warn the cubs of danger. When a threat is nearby, the mother makes a loud braying or a chuffing sound. Chuffing is a sharp, puffing sound like a steam engine.

A Polar Bear growling

Protecting her young

Cubs play fighting

Polar Bears show affection with body language.

Mother Polar Bears comfort and protect cubs by nuzzling them or touching their bodies with their paws. These same gestures can also be used to scold their young.

When a male cub wants to play with another cub, he approaches the other cub with his head downs before touching the other cub on the mouth or neck with his own mouth.

To begin playtime, Polar Bears stand on their hind legs and push each other over with their front paws.

7 Cool Polar Bear Facts:

1. The word Arctic comes from the Greek word for Bear. The word Antarctic comes from the Greek meaning "without Bear", the opposite.

2. Polar Bears have almost the same body temperature as humans -- 98.6°F (37°C).

3. A Polar Bear's liver contains 10 times more Vitamin A than any other animal on earth — their liver has evolved to allow them to process and eat all of the Seal fat they need to stay alive.

4. Polar Bears and Penguins can never meet. Polar Bears live in the Arctic around the North Pole and Penguins live in the Antarctic around the South Pole.

5. A group of Polar Bears is called a sleuth or a pack.

6. Feb 27th is International Polar Bear Day.

7. The first Coca-Cola advertisement to feature Polar Bears was in France - in 1922.

Polar Bear Senses

SMELL

Polar Bears have a great sense of smell, which they use to find prey.

They rely more on their sense of smell than any of their other senses when hunting.

A Polar Bear can sniff out a Seal on the ice 20 miles (32 km) away. They can smell a Seal's breathing hole in the ice more than .5 mile (800 m) away.

A Polar Bear sniffing the air

HEARING

A Polar Bears's hearing is about as good as that of a Human.

Polar Bear Senses

SIGHT

Polar Bears have special adaptations that help them to see underwater.

Like many other Marine Mammals, they have a clear inner "eyelid" called a nictitating membrane, that protects their eyes. This special membrane acts as a second lens for the eye to see more clearly when they are underwater. It also protects them from blowing snow and shields their eyes from the Sun's ultraviolet light.

During the day, out on the ice, a Polar Bear's sense of sight is about as good as that of a Human. At night, a Polar Bear's sense of sight is far better than that of Human.

A Polar Bear underwater

Sharp Teeth - Powerful Bite

Big Sharp Teeth

Polar Bears have a mouth full of 42 extremely sharp teeth. They use their teeth for catching food and for aggressive behavior. Since they are meat eaters, they need their teeth to kill their prey, as well as to eat it.

Their teeth are longer and sharper than those of the Brown Bear. Polar Bears use their sharp teeth to grasp their prey, and to tear off pieces of meat, tough hides and blubber.

With a bite force of 1200 pounds per square inch, Polar Bears have a bite force that places them in the Top 10 Most Powerful Bites in the Animal Kingdom. A Human has a bite force of only about 150 pounds per square inch, 8 times less powerful.

GIANT Paws and Claws

Polar Bear claws are shorter and sharper than Brown Bear claws, measuring up to 4 inches (10 cm) long.

Polar Bear claws are also very thick, sharp and curved.

They use their claws to grip frozen sea ice or grab onto slippery prey, like a Ringed Seal.

Big paws
Big claws

The paw of a Polar Bear is very wide and can measure about 12 inches (30 cm) across.

Their wide paws help Polar Bears spread out their weight, so they can walk on thin ice without falling through.

Walking on thin ice

Polar Bears have slightly webbed feet that helps them swim. When swimming, Polar Bears use their huge front paws as paddles to pull them through the water. They use their back paws as rudders to help steer them where they want to go.

On the underside of their paws, the soles of their feet, Polar Bears have bumpy black pads. The bumps help the Polar Bear grip the ice so that it doesn't slip.

Bumpy black foot pads on a sleeping Bear

Polar Bear Cubs

The months of March through May is the Polar Bear breeding season. Males pick up the scent of females and track them across the ice. Often, a few males battle to mate with a female.

The winner stays with the female for about a week. After that time, the male leaves the female. Males do not help to care for the cubs.

For the next 4 months, the female Polar Bear eats enough food to prepare for a long fast, often gaining more than 400 pounds (181 kg), nearly doubling her body weight.

In the Fall she builds a den by burrowing into the snow or permafrost to create a snow cave - just large enough for her to turn around in. She then waits for the snow to close the entrance tunnel. Pregnant Polar Bears dig deep dens to hibernate and to keep themselves warm in the harsh Arctic Winters.

A Polar Bear Den in the snow

Polar Bear Cubs - Twins

The gestation period is about 8 months. Sometime between November and January, the sow gives birth. There are usually 2 or 3 cubs. Twins are the most common.

Newborn Polar Bears are 12 - 14 inches (30 - 35 cm) long and weigh about 1 pound (.5 kg). They are blind, toothless and covered with short, soft fur. They are completely dependent on their mother for warmth and food.

They grow rapidly on their mother's rich milk (31% fat). She nurses them until early Spring, when she breaks open the entrance to the den, and they leave the den. By now the cubs weigh about 22 - 33 pounds (10 - 15 kg).

First the cubs take a few weeks to learn to move about, then the mother and cubs return to the ice flows so that she can hunt. The female Polar Bear hunts for Seals for herself, and her cubs learn to hunt by watching her.

Polar Bear Cubs

Female Polar Bears protect and care for their young by nursing them and providing nourishment from the time they are born until they are weaned at 1.5 to 2.5 years of age.

The female is not only affectionate but also protective. Dangers include Wolves and Polar Bear males, who sometimes attack and eat the cubs.

The mother abandons or drives away the cubs after they are weaned and she is ready to mate again.

Around the age of 4 or 5 the female Polar Bear can start having cubs.

On average, female Polar Bears produce 5 litters during their entire lives. This rate is the lowest among all mammals on Earth.

Polar Bear mom and cubs

Catching a ride on mom's back

Exploring

Do all Polar Bears Hibernate?

Male Polar Bears generally do not hibernate. They remain active for most of the year.

Only pregnant female Polar Bears hibernate and build dens to give birth to and to raise their young, just like Black Bears, Brown Bears and other Bears.

Polar Bears' state of hibernation is different from other animals' hibernation periods. Other animals drop their body temperature during their hibernation periods, but Polar Bears do not. Polar Bears maintain their body temperature while reducing their need for food. A higher body temperature is needed to nurse her cubs. For the entire hibernation period, mother Polar Bears live off the fat they have built up in their bodies.

Female Polar Bear and Cubs in their den

Are Polar Bears good swimmers?

Polar Bears are strong swimmers. They swim across bays or wide stretches of open water. Because they spend so much time in the water, Polar Bears are considered to be Marine Mammals.

A Polar Bear's front paws propel them through the water dog-paddle style.

A thick layer of fat, up to 4 inches (10.15 cm) thick, keeps the Polar Bear warm while swimming in cold water.

Going for a swim

Polar Bears can reach a speed of 6 mph (10 km/h) when swimming. When underwater, a Polar Bear's nostrils close.

They can swim for many hours at a time over long distances. Scientists have recorded Polar Bears regularly swimming over 30 miles (48 kilometers). In one case, a Polar Bear swam as far as 220 miles (354 km) in a one stretch. Cubs do not have the stamina and strength to swim long distances.

Polar Bears are solitary animals

Polar Bears prefer to live by themselves. Male and female Polar Bears only meet up to mate. This is only for a short period of time of a week or two. After this they return to their solitary life styles.

Only females with cubs live with other Polar Bears - their young.

Even in zoo settings in which two or more Polar Bears share a space, they stick to different areas of their enclosure away from one another.

How much do Polar Bears sleep?

Just like Humans, most Polar Bears sleep for 7 to 8 hours at a stretch. They take naps too.

Sleeping on the ice

Polar Bears curl up, sometimes using a block of ice or an outstretched paw as a pillow. Polar Bars sleep on the open ground. They dig pits in gravel and sand at shorelines, or dig shallow areas in the snow or beneath protected ridges. Once inside these protective hollows, they turn their backs to the wind. During blizzards, the snow covers and insulates the Bears from the cold.

The Polar Bear's main prey, the Seal, is most active at night. So Polar Bears will rest at the times when their prey is not active. Also, hunting takes energy, so Polar Bears nap often to help conserve their energy.

How have Polar Bears adapted to their environment?

Small ears reduce heat loss in the cold

Super sense of smell helps to find prey

Razor sharp Canine teeth to kill prey

Strong legs for swimming

Sharp claws to grab prey and for grip on ice

Thick fur for insulation and camouflage

A short tail helps reduce heat loss

Thick layer of fat helps insulate and stores energy

Paw pads and fur on the soles of the feet for grip and insulation

Large feet to spread weight on snow and ice

Polar Bears like to keep clean

Polar Bears like to be clean and dry because matted, dirty and wet fur is a bad insulator from the cold.

In Summer, after eating, Polar Bears get into the water and clean off. They lick their paws, chests, and muzzles. They then shake off the water and dry themselves by rubbing their fur in the snow.

In Winter, Polar Bears clean themselves mainly with with snow and with water if it is available. They also rub their heads in the snow, push forwards while lying on their on their stomachs, and they roll on their backs in the snow.

Polar Bears remove small pieces of ice from their paws to make walking more comfortable.

Mother Polar Bears lick their cubs to keep them clean. Cubs also lick themselves and each other.

Polar Bears are Athletes

Polar Bears can sprint for short distances at speeds as fast as 30 miles per hour (40 km/h). That is as fast as the fastest Human sprinters . Younger, leaner bears are the best runners. They can cover 1.25 miles (2 km) without stopping. Older, larger bears cannot run nearly as far or they will quickly overheat.

Polar Bears are long distance wanderers, capable of walking 20 miles (32 km) or more in a single day. And they can do this for many days in row across jumbled up ice and snow. Polar Bears have been tracked walking 50 miles (80 km) in about 24 hours and up to 700 miles (1,125 km) in a single year.

Walking Bears expend 13 times more energy than resting Bears. This partly explains why, when hunting, Polar Bears prefer a long, patient wait for a Seal to surface at a breathing hole in the sea ice.

MORE Cool Polar Bear Facts:

1. Polar Bears are great mothers. A study found that female Polar Bears will sometimes adopt abandoned cubs into their own families.

2. Some researchers believe that Polar Bears could be as smart as some Apes, which makes them one of the most intelligent animals in the world.

3. Licence plates in Canada's Northwest Territories are shaped like Polar Bears.

4. Churchill in Manitoba Province, Canada is the Polar Bear capital of the world. In Fall, there are so many Bears in the area that residents of the town leave their cars unlocked. If any pedestrians encounter a Polar Bear in the street, they will have a place to escape to.

5. Polar Bears are the most aggressive of all Bears

6. Polar Bears find each other with smelly footprints. With each step, they leave chemical deposits from their foot pads on the ice. This creates a scent trail in their footprints that other Bears can sniff. This helps them to find a mate, or avoid competition.

HUMAN THREATS

More Humans in the Arctic

Humans are the Polar Bears only predator. All across the Arctic, people are moving in to mine oil and coal and there is less space for the Polar Bear to live.

Oil Pollution

Oil spills can be very dangerous. A Polar Bear with oil on its coat cannot regulate its body temperature properly. If the Bear eats the oil while grooming itself, it could die.

Pollution in the Food Chain

Manmade pollution in the sea is also a cause of death. At each stage of the food chain, pollutants become more concentrated. By the end of the food chain, when the Polar Bear eats the Seal, it could be deadly to the Bear.

THANKS FOR READING!

Please leave a review at your favorite bookseller's website like www.Amazon.com - Please share with others what you liked about this book.

Visit www.TJRob.com to get a FREE eBook and to learn about other exciting books by TJ Rob:

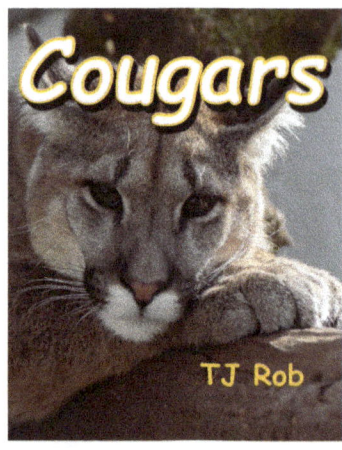

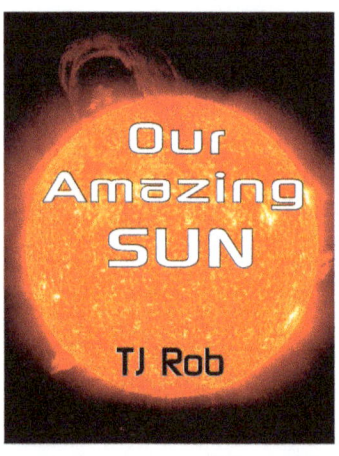

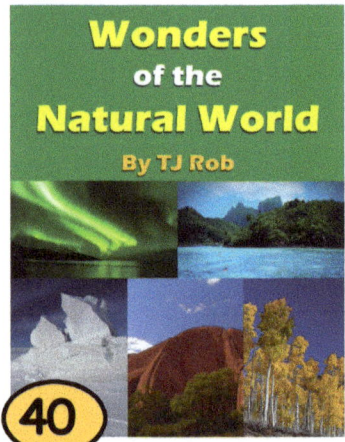
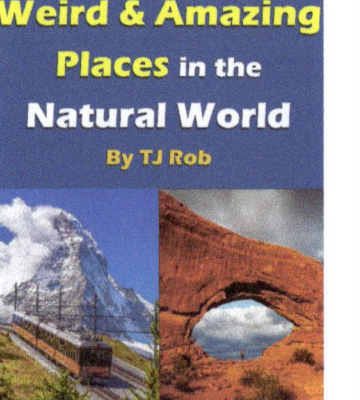
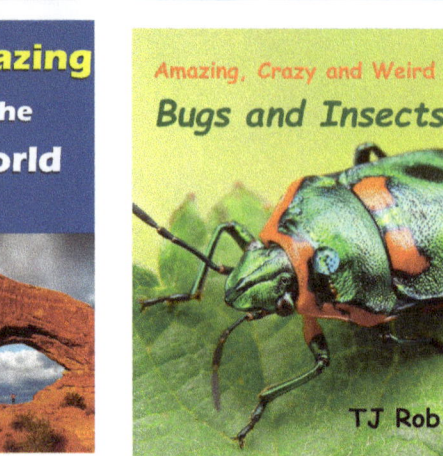

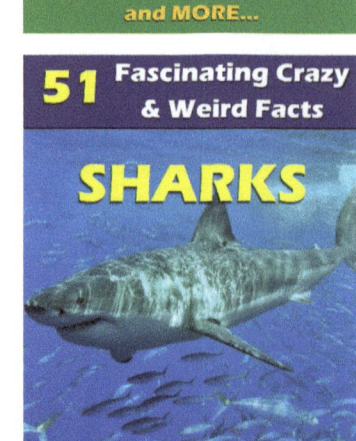

www.ingramcontent.com/pod-product-compliance
Lightning Source LLC
Chambersburg PA
CBHW040005080526
44586CB00027B/2887